Mobiles & Other Paper Windcatchers

Noel Fiarotta & Phyllis Fiarotta

STERLING PUBLISHING CO., INC.
NEW YORK

Edited by Jeanette Green

Library of Congress Cataloging-in-Publication Data

Fiarotta, Phyllis.
    Mobiles & other paper windcatchers / by Phyllis Fiarotta and Noel
Fiarotta.
        p.   cm.
    Includes index.
    ISBN 0-8069-8106-7
    1. Mobiles (Sculpture)   2. Paper work.   I. Fiarotta, Noel.
II. Title.
TT899.F53   1996
731'.55—dc20   96-11997

Published by Sterling Publishing Company, Inc.
387 Park Avenue South, New York, N.Y. 10016
© 1996 by Phyllis Fiarotta and Noel Fiarotta
Distributed in Canada by Sterling Publishing
% Canadian Manda Group, One Atlantic Avenue, Suite 105
Toronto, Ontario, Canada M6K 3E7
Distributed in Great Britain and Europe by Cassell PLC
Wellington House, l25 Strand, London WC2R 0BB, England
Distributed in Australia by Capricorn Link (Australia) Pty Ltd.
P.O. Box 6651, Baulkham Hills, Business Centre, NSW 2153, Australia
Printed in Hong Kong
All rights reserved

Sterling ISBN 0-8069-8106-7

CONTENTS

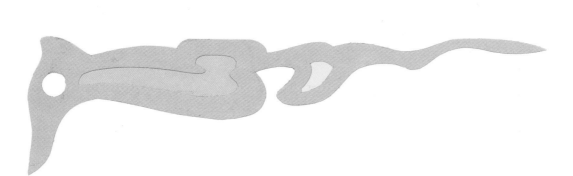

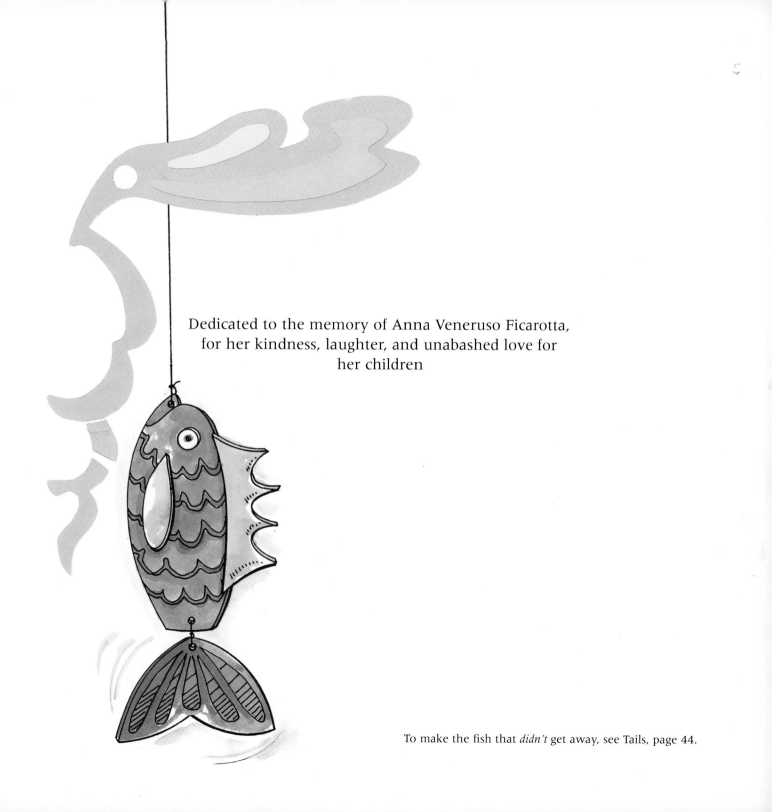

Dedicated to the memory of Anna Veneruso Ficarotta,
for her kindness, laughter, and unabashed love for
her children

To make the fish that *didn't* get away, see Tails, page 44.

BLOWING IN THE WIND

Wind instruments that make music, windjammers that sail seas, and the human windpipe that gives us voice and breath depend upon a flow of air—what we call wind—to operate. Wind drives engines great and small. Windmills create energy and grind grain into flour, while simple wind chimes produce pleasing sound.

Fabric windcatchers assume different forms—a boat's sails, airport wind socks, and national banners. In Siberia colorful strips of cloth are tied to defoliated winter trees to flutter in cold winds off Lake Baikal, and in Tibet prayer flags and ribbons hang from poles and decorate mountain shrines.

Windcatchers made of paper appeared in China after the development of paper in 250 B.C. The Chinese crafted kites to rise aloft into upper air currents and paper lanterns to sway in lower whiffs. Nearly all cultures have developed paper garlands, pennants, and flags to add colorful overhead movement during festivals. From Italy comes confetti and from Mexico, fringed and tasseled piñatas. And what *bon voyage* would be complete without curlicue streamers trailing off the ship's deck?

Along with summer's gentle breezes, stiff offshore gusts, and hurling hurricanes, air movement (little winds) can come from the draft from a closing door, a short puff of breath, or a steady flow from an electric fan.

Hang these paper mobiles and windcatchers anywhere air moves freely—from a room or porch ceiling; in a window or door; on poles, trellises, outdoor or indoor trees, and lines of rope.

These mobiles and other paper windcatchers will appeal to both adults and children. Many of the mobiles are especially designed for children, like the Three Little Kittens, Pirate's Treasure, and Baseball. Because these projects are simple, children can create them on their own or work with adult guidance. Use sturdier materials or waterproof the project if you want more permanent displays. As you begin this adventure into the whimsical world of paper mobiles and windcatchers, may your breezes be playful and your scissors sharp.

BASIC
INFORMATION

Choose the proper weight strings: button thread or invisible sewing thread, tatting or needle-craft string, fishing line, yarn, and cords. Choose origami, construction, sturdy craft papers, or poster board as lightweight cardboard. For outdoor use, color with indelible markers and fabric paints (in bottles), and use waterproof glue. For inclement weather, bring the mobile or windcatcher inside.

PLASTIC DRINKING STRAWS (A) Make a pole by pinching the ends of straws and pushing them into the open end of other straws. To keep string in place, cut a small slit (arrow) and wedge the string into it. Pinch a straw flat before punching out a hole.

HOLES (B) A paper punch makes a large, clean hole in paper. Also use a large nail.

REINFORCEMENT (C) To strengthen a hole, reinforce it with a line of glue or a lick-on loose-leaf (hole) reinforcer.

TIED CUTOUTS (D) For a single string, tie one end into a hole. For a double string, tie the middle of the string into the hole.

GLUED CUTOUTS (E) Cut two matching shapes from folded paper. Tape string on the center of a shape. Add glue and place the second shape on top of the first.

DIVERSE CUTOUTS (F) Add tied and glued shapes to string, along with tied-on beads.

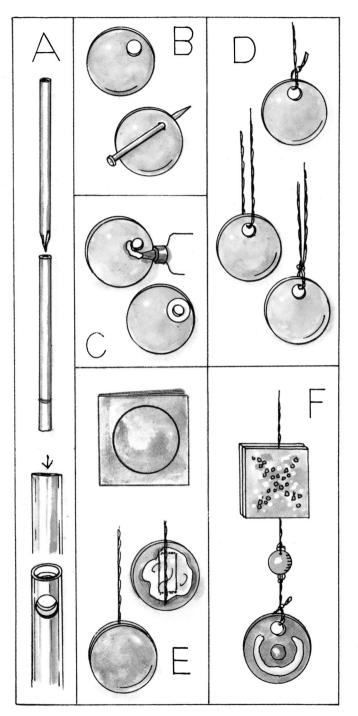

STABILITY (G) Feed string through two holes rather than one, to minimize turning.

SPIN (H) Tie a small paper circle, a paper clip, small macaroni, button, or bead to string. Feed the string through a hole made in the middle of a paper shape.

BALANCE (I) Tape cord at different points along the top edge of a completed hanging until you find the balance point. Permanently secure in place.

SCOOPS (J) Curl opposite sides of a paper shape, facing in the opposite direction to encourage the shape to spin.

SUBSTITUTIONS (K) (not shown) Use wooden dowels in place of straws. Make ribbon flags and wind socks in lightweight fabric. Use oil cloth or pliable plastic for cutout shapes. Use fabric ribbon instead of crepe-paper streamers.

WATERPROOFING (L) (not shown) Spray on a fabric stain-resister or rub in cooking oil. Rub on canning paraffin or brush on melted paraffin. Oiled and wax-soaked paper will darken.

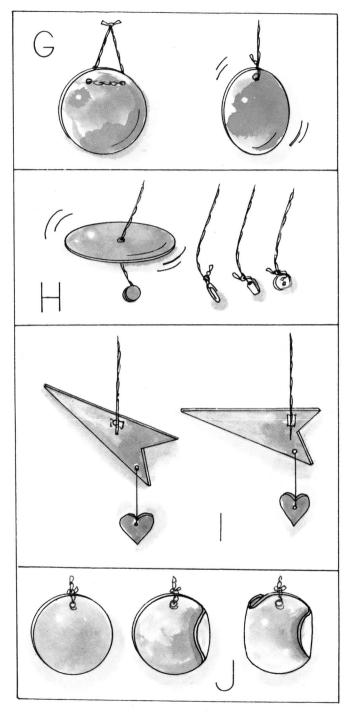

ON A STRING

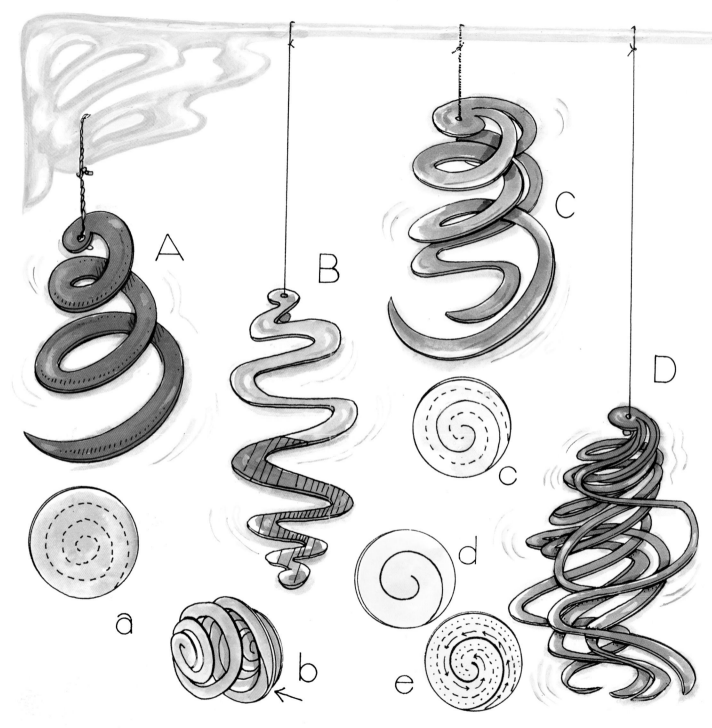

A

B

C

D

a

b

c

d

e

COILS

SUPPLIES: Construction paper, round plate, pencil, scissors, paper punch, glue or paste, string, button or paper clip, plastic straws, play clay, straight pin, small tin can, salt.

SINGLE CUT (A)

1. Trace around a dish on paper. Cut out.

2. Cut a spiral into the circle beginning at the edge and moving toward the center (a).

3. Punch a hole in the center of the coil.

4. Hang the coil with string tied to a button.

TWO COLOR (B)
Make two single coils. Glue the ends of the coils together (b).

TWO CUTS (C)
Make two spiral cuts into a circle. Study solid and broken lines (c).

MULTIPLE CUTS (D)
Make three or four separate spiral cuts into a circle (d and e).

STANDING COIL (E)

1. Tape a drawing around a can (f).

2. Pinch the end of a straw and push it into the end of another straw.

3. Push clay into the top of the double straw (arrow in g).

4. Stand the straw in a can filled with salt.

5. Push a straight pin through the middle of the coil and into the clay.

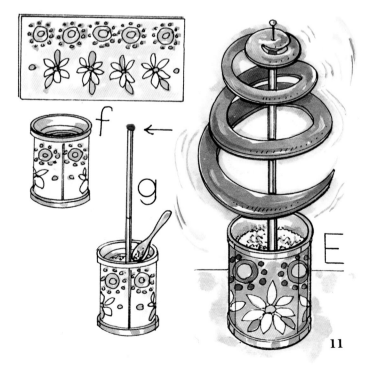

11

LOOPS

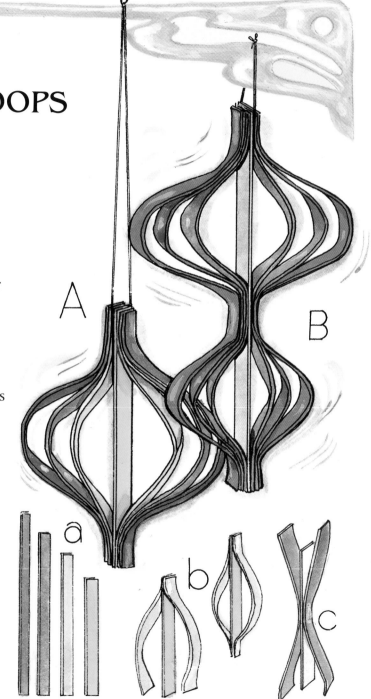

SUPPLIES: Construction paper, scissors, paste, string.

SINGLE LOOPS (A)

1. Cut four strips of paper, each a little longer than the last (a). Cut a second set of strips the same size as the first.

2. Paste the ends of the second longest strips to the ends of the shortest strip (b).

3. Paste on the remaining longest sets of strips to the second shortest strips, as above.

4. Hang with string.

DOUBLE LOOPS (B)

1. Cut strips as above, but make each set much longer than the shortest strip.

2. First paste the strips together at their middle points (c) before pasting the ends together.

RINGS

SUPPLIES: Construction paper, compass, scissors, string, glue or tape.

1. Using a compass, draw many rings on two different colored sheets of paper.

2. Fold each paper in half across the hole made by the compass point (a).

3. Cut out the rings. Open (b).

4. On a flat surface, arrange three or more rings each inside the other. The rings should not touch each other.

5. Lay string across the middle of the rings. Glue or tape in place (arrow in c).

13

WEB

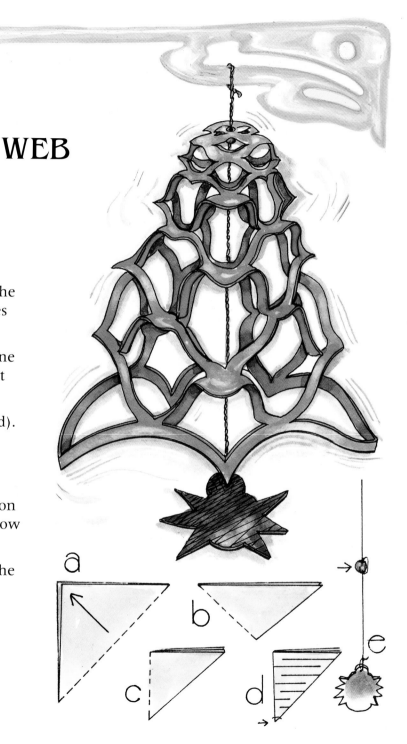

SUPPLIES: Construction paper, scissors, string, button or paper clip.

1. Fold a large paper square in half along the diagonal (a). Fold in half two more times (b and c).

2. Cut slits into the folded edges, first on one side, then on the other (study d). Do not cut through the folded edges.

3. Cut off a tiny bit of the point (arrow in d).

4. Open the paper. Pull out to form a web.

5. Draw a spider on paper. Cut out.

6. Tie string to the spider (e). Tie a button on the string a little up from the spider (arrow in e).

7. Feed the string inside the web and out the hole at the top.

CURTAIN

SUPPLIES: Construction paper, pencil, scissors, tape, glue or paste, string.

1. Draw circles, triangles, or other shapes about the same size on colored paper. Cut out.

2. Cut several long strings the same size. The more strings, the wider the curtain.

3. Tape shapes to the strings. Glue their matching shapes onto them (see diagram).

4. You can add this curtain to a doorway or window or place it across the corner of a room. Tie strings to an old broom and hang or tape the individual strings to a surface.

TOTEM POLE

SUPPLIES: Colored poster board, pencil, construction paper, scissors, crayons or markers, cord, tape.

1. Draw three large animal heads on poster board. The stylized animals shown starting at the top, are an eagle, wolf, and beaver. They are from an authentic totem pole. Also draw wings for the eagle. Cut out.

2. Draw and decorate the faces and wings with crayons or markers. Decorate the backs of the heads (see diagram).

3. Lay a long cord down the middle of the back of the animals. Tape in place.

ORNAMENTS

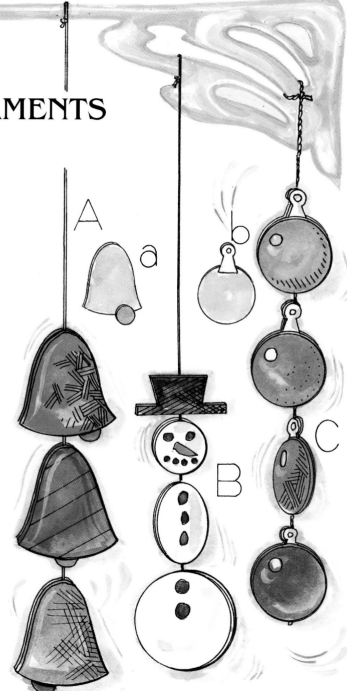

SUPPLIES: Construction paper, pencil, scissors, glue or paste, crayons or markers, paper hangers, string.

BELLS (A)

1. Cut two paper bells the same size (see page 7, E). Cut out.

2. Glue a small paper circle to one of every two bells (a).

3. Tape the bells with the circles to a string. Glue their matching shapes on them.

4. Glue on glitter, if you wish.

SNOWMAN (B)

Attach a paper hat and snowballs on a string, as you did the bells. Draw a face and buttons with crayons or markers.

CHRISTMAS BALLS (C)

Attach paper balls to a string with a small paper hanger between them (b).

FLAGS

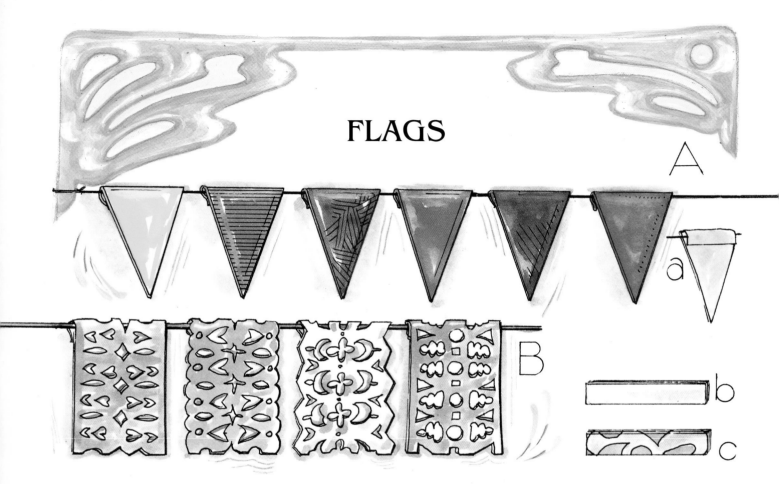

SUPPLIES: Construction paper, white or colored tissue paper, pencil, ruler, scissors, cord, glue or paste, strong tape.

PENNANTS (A)

1. Draw triangles the same size on paper with a pencil and ruler. Cut them out.

2. Fold the top of the pennants over a long cord (a). Glue in place.

3. String the flags across a room or an outside patio. Attach with tape or tie in place.

PAPER CUTS (B)

1. Fold tissue-paper rectangles of the same size in half several times (b).

2. Cut out shapes along the folded sides (c).

3. Fold the tops of the opened flags over a long cord. Glue in place.

SENTIMENTS

SUPPLIES: Construction paper, pencil, ruler, scissors, crayons or markers, paper punch, string, cord, plastic straws.

HANGING LETTERS (A)

1. Cut standard-size sheets of paper in half across the widths.

2. In a light pencil line, draw a letter on each rectangle. Cut out.

3. If you wish, draw decorations on the letters with crayons or markers.

4. Punch a hole into the middle of each letter near the top. The hole will be further down on letters like H and Y.

5. Tie string to the letters. Tie the letters to a long cord.

ROCKING LETTERS (B)

1. Draw and cut out letters as above.

2. Tape a small piece of drinking straw to the back of each letter near the top (see diagram for Y).

3. Feed string though the straws.

19

SINGLE

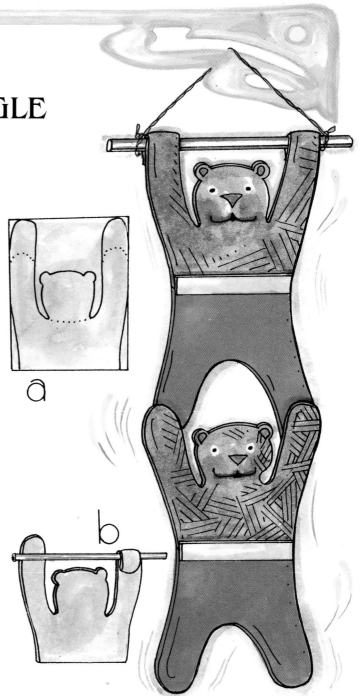

SUPPLIES: Plastic straws, string, construction paper, scissors, glue or paste, crayons or markers.

MOBILE
Tie string to the ends of a straw.

ACROBAT BEARS
1. Cut a sheet of brown paper and a sheet of colored paper in half across the width.

2. Draw the upper half of the bears on brown paper and the lower half (legs) on colored paper. Draw the legs like the upper bear but without the head (see dotted lines in a). Cut out.

3. Glue the legs to the upper bear. Glue on paper belts.

4. Glue the hands of one bear to the feet of the other.

5. Fold the hands of the top bear over the straw (b). Glue in place.

a

b

DOUBLE

SUPPLIES: Plastic straws, string, construction paper, pencil, scissors, crayons or markers, glue or paste, paper punch.

MOBILE

1. Pinch the end of a straw and push it into the end of another straw.

2. Attach a single straw to the double straw, with string tied to their middles.

3. To hang, tie string to the middle of the double straw.

BIRDS

1. Cut pink and white paper into four equal parts (a). Fold each in half.

2. Draw half a heart on the fold of each paper (b). Cut out.

3. On each white heart, cut a small slit into the fold (arrow in c). Draw wing designs.

4. On each pink heart, cut an upward slit into the folded edge (arrow in d). Draw eyes. Glue on a paper beak.

5. To make the birds, fit the slits of the pink and white hearts into each other.

6. Punch a hole into each bird for hanging.

7. Tie the birds to the mobile with string.

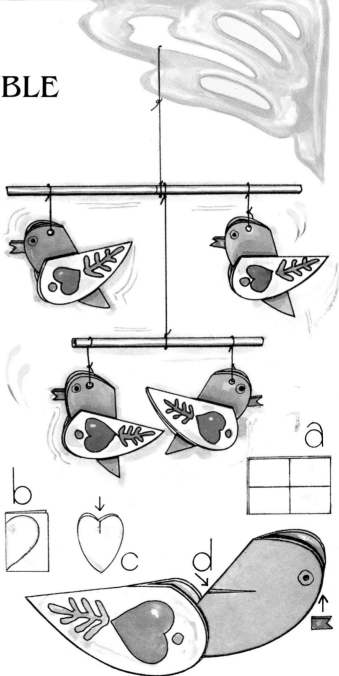

CRISSCROSS

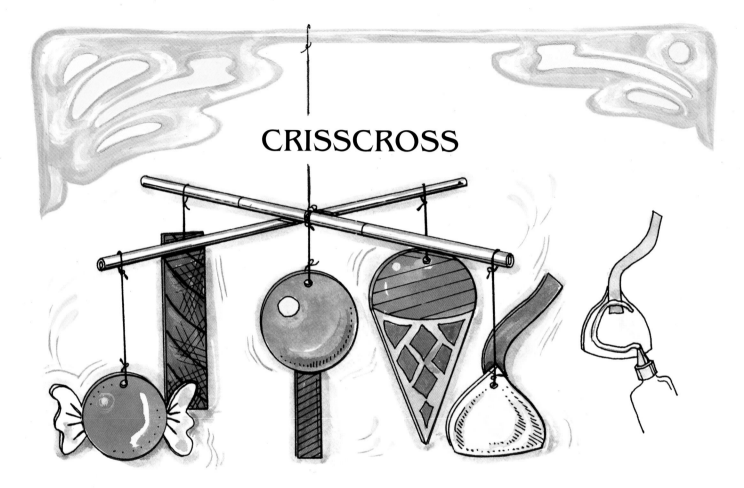

SUPPLIES: Plastic straws, string, construction, paper, crayons or markers, scissors, glue or paste, paper punch.

MOBILE

1. Pinch the end of a straw and push it into the end of another straw. Make two.

2. Crisscross the double straws at their middles. Tie together.

3. To hang, tie string to the middle of the crossed straws.

SWEETS

1. Draw on colored paper five sweet treats. Shown are a sour ball, a licorice stick, a lollipop, an ice cream cone, and a chocolate drop. Cut out. Glue a second, matching sweet to the first if you want two finished sides.

2. Punch a hole into each sweet for hanging.

3. Tie the sweets to the mobile with string.

TRIPLE

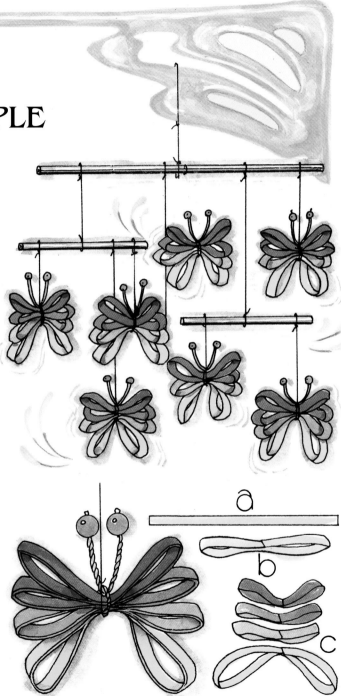

SUPPLIES: Plastic straws, string, construction paper, scissors, glue or paste, pipe cleaners, beads.

MOBILE
1. Pinch the end of a straw and push it into the end of another straw.

2. Attach a single straw to the double straw, with string tied to their middles.

3. To hang, tie string to the middle of the double straw.

BUTTERFLIES
1. For each butterfly, cut four paper strips (a). They should be narrow and very long.

2. Glue the ends of each strip to the middle point, creating two loops (b).

3. To make a butterfly, glue four looped strips together at their middles (c).

4. Wrap a pipe cleaner around each butterfly for antennae. Push beads onto the ends of the pipe cleaner.

5. Tie butterflies to the mobile with string.

LADDER

SUPPLIES: Plastic straws, cord, white paper, pencil, scissors, waxed paper, glue, glitter, paper punch, string.

MOBILE

1. Pinch the end of a straw and push it into the end of another straw. Make four.

2. Attach the double straws together with cord tied to their middles (see illustration).

3. To hang, tie cord to the middle of the top straw.

FIREWORKS

1. Draw fireworks on white paper. Cut out.

2. Place the fireworks on waxed paper.

3. Draw designs on each firework with glue (a).

4. Sprinkle glitter onto the glue (b). Dry.

5. Punch a hole into each firework for hanging.

6. Tie fireworks to the mobile with string.

ZIGZAG

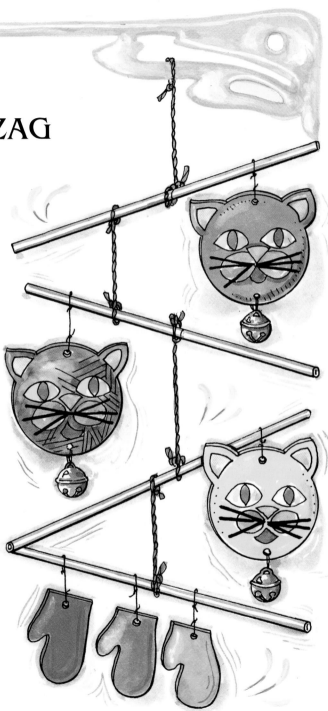

SUPPLIES: Plastic straws, cord, construction paper, crayons or markers, scissors, paper punch, small jingle bells, string.

MOBILE
1. Pinch the end of a straw and push it into the end of another straw. Make four.

2. Tie the double straws to each other in a left-right pattern, as shown.

3. To hang, tie cord to the middle of the top straw.

THREE LITTLE KITTENS
1. Draw three kittens and mittens on paper. Cut out.

2. Punch holes into the top and bottom of each kitten. Punch holes into the mittens.

3. Tie bells to the bottom of each kitten.

4. Tie kittens and mittens to the mobile with string.

5. Hang. If the mobile hangs lopsided, adjust the attachment cords for the zigzag balance you want.

GRADUATED

SUPPLIES: Plastic straws, cord, construction paper, crayons or markers, scissors, paste, paper punch, string, garland.

MOBILE

1. Pinch the end of a straw and push it into the end of another straw. Make several.

2. A single straw is the top branch. The lower branches are double straws, each cut shorter than the other.

3. Tie the straws together at their middles with cord, as shown.

4. To hang, tie cord to the middle of the top straw.

DECORATIONS

1. Draw balls, a star, a tree base, and gift boxes on colored paper. Cut out.

2. Punch a hole into each decoration.

3. Tie decorations to the tree with string, as shown. Add garland to complete the Christmas tree.

STAR-SHAPES

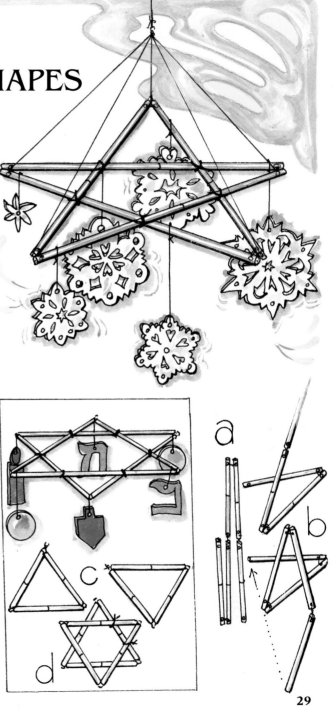

SUPPLIES: Plastic straws, paper punch, string, paper doilies, construction paper, compass, pencil, scissors, string.

FIVE-POINT STAR MOBILE

1. Pinch the end of a straw and push it into the end of another straw. Make five.

2. Press the ends of the straws flat and punch holes into them with a punch.

3. Tie the straws together in a row, with string threaded through the holes (a).

4. Crisscross the straws to form a star (b). Tie the end together. Also tie the straws together where they cross.

5. To hang, tie cord to the points, then tie all strings together securely.

SIX-POINT STAR MOBILE

1. Tie three double straws together forming a triangle (d). Make two.

2. Tie the triangles together forming a star.

3. To hang, tie cord to the points, then tie all strings together securely.

ORNAMENTS

With string, hang snowflakes cut from doilies on the five-point star or Chanukah symbols cut from paper on the six-point star.

ARCS

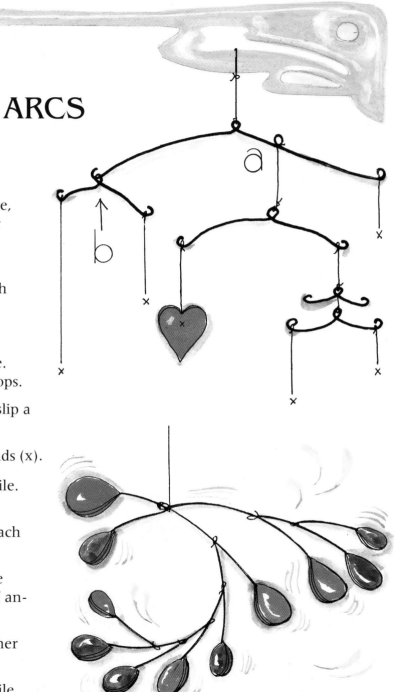

SUPPLIES: Medium- or heavy-gauge wire, scissors, construction paper, string, glue or paste.

SEPARATE SUPPORTS

1. Cut different lengths of wire. Bend each into an arc (curve).

2. Curl the ends of each wire.

3. Make a loop in the middle of each wire. On longer wires, you can make two loops.

4. Attach arcs together with string (a) or slip a loop onto a curled end (b).

5. Hang paper designs from the curved ends (x).

6. To hang, tie cord to the top of the mobile.

INTERCONNECTED SUPPORTS

1. Cut wire into different lengths. Bend each into an arc (curve).

2. Attach the arcs together by twisting the end of one tightly around the center of another (study the mobile).

3. Glue two matching paper shapes together with a wire end between them.

4. To hang, tie cord to the top of the mobile.

30

CREATIVE
MOBILES

OFF BALANCE

SUPPLIES: Heavy cardboard, colored poster board, construction paper, pencil, crayons or markers, scissors, glue or paste, paper punch, string, cord.

GEOMETRIC (A)

1. Draw triangles on paper. Cut out.

2. Punch holes into the triangles for hanging.

3. Tie the triangles together with string.

4. Cut a long triangle from cardboard.

5. Tie or tape the connected triangles to the narrow point of the cardboard triangle.

6. To hang the mobile, keep taping a piece of cord to different points along the top of the cardboard triangle (see diagram). When the mobile hangs straight, make a hole at that point. Tie cord into the hole.

BASEBALL (B)

1. On poster board, draw a baseball bat. On paper, use a compass to draw a ball and draw a star with many points. Cut out.

2. Draw the name of a baseball team on the bat and stitches on the ball.

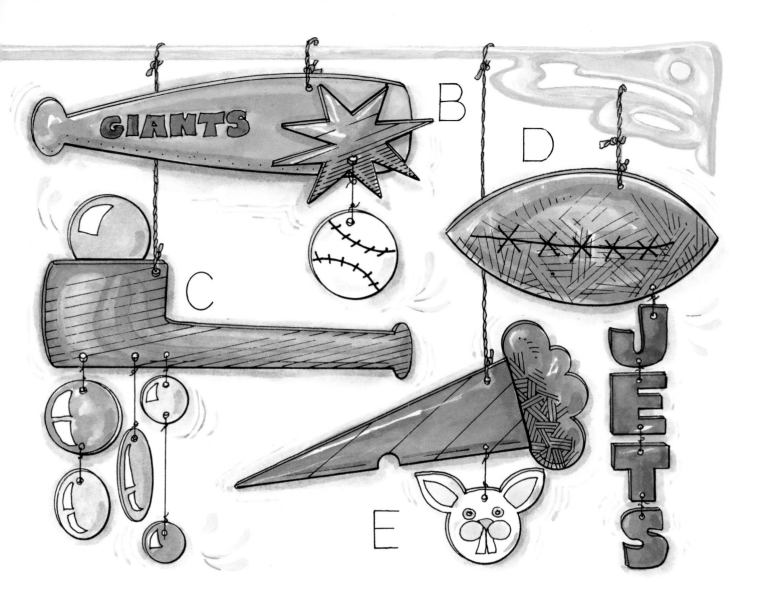

3. Punch holes into the star and ball. Tie together with string as shown.

4. Glue the star on the end of the bat.

5. Hang the mobile as described in Geometric.

BUBBLE PIPE (C), FOOTBALL (D), CARROT (E)

Make a bubble pipe with bubbles, a football with a team name, and a carrot with a bunny, as you did the Baseball.

TWIG

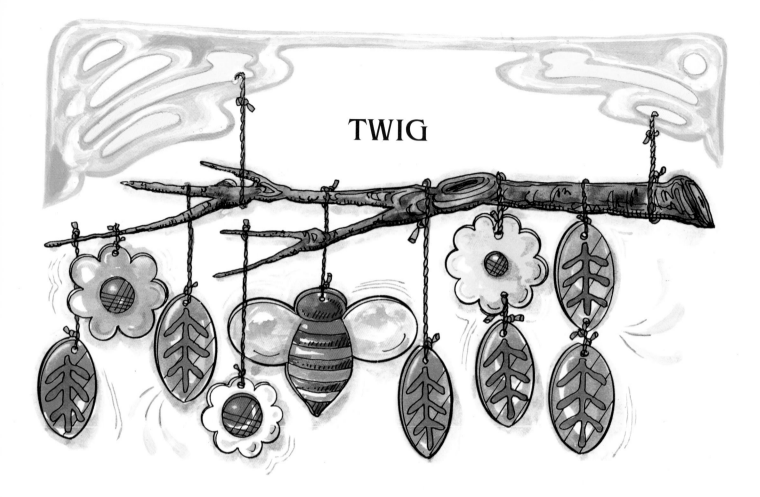

SUPPLIES: Twig, construction paper, crayons or markers, scissors, paper punch, cord.

1. Draw leaves, flowers, and a bumble bee on paper. Cut out.

2. Punch holes into the cutouts for hanging.

3. With string, tie the cutouts to the twig as well as to each other.

4. To hang the mobile, tie cord to both ends of the twig.

BOX

SUPPLIES: Cereal box, scissors, tape, pencil, construction paper, crayons or markers, glue or paste, compass, photographs, string.

1. Tape closed the open end of a cereal box after you cut away one long side (a).

2. Cut a slit into each corner (arrows in a).

3. To form a peak, first fold over the short sides (arrow in b), then the long sides. Tape the long sides together to form a house (b).

4. Trace the front, back, sides, and bottom of the box on paper. Cut out.

5. Glue the cutouts on the house (c and d).

6. Glue on a door, windows, and bushes. Draw on shingles and window panes.

7. Cut family photographs into circles. Cut a matching paper circle for each.

8. Glue a photo to a paper circle with the end of a piece of string between them.

9. Tape strings of photos to the bottom of the house (e).

10. To hang the mobile, feed cord under the roof and knot the ends.

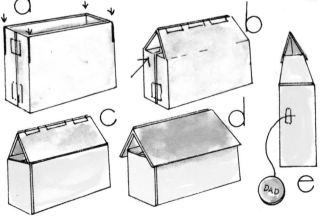

HANGER

A

B

SUPPLIES: Coat hanger, scissors, construction paper, crayons or markers, string, ribbon.

PIRATE'S TREASURE (A)

1. Draw a pirate, sword, treasure chest, and skull and crossbones on paper. Cut out.

2. Punch holes into the cutouts for hanging.

3. With string, tie the cutouts on a hanger.

4. Hang the mobile by the hook.

FLYING FISH (B)

1. Wrap ribbon around a hanger.

2. Draw fish and bubbles on paper. Cut out.

3. Punch holes into the cutouts for hanging.

4. With string, tie the fish to the hanger.

5. Tie on paper bubbles glued to string and ribbon seaweed.

6. Hang the mobile by the hook.

HOOP

SUPPLIES: Embroidery hoop, construction paper, pencil, scissors, paper punch, beads, string.

1. Cut small paper rectangles in Valentine's Day colors. Fold each in half.

2. Draw half a heart on the fold of each paper with a pencil (see diagram).

3. Draw half a heart inside the hearts. The bottom stops a little away from the fold (arrow in diagram).

4. Cut along all drawn lines.

5. Open the hearts. Push out the inside hearts.

6. Punch holes into the hearts for hanging.

7. Tie beads and hearts to different lengths of string.

8. Tie hearts to a hoop, each hanging a little lower than the last.

9. To hang the mobile, tie cord to three or four points on the hoop.

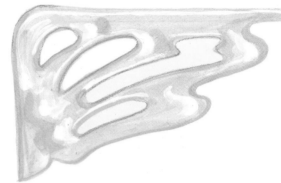

PLATE

SUPPLIES: Sturdy white paper plate, pencil, cord, paper clip, construction paper, scissors, glue or paste, paper punch, string.

1. Draw the sun, stars, planets, and a rocket ship on paper. Cut out.

2. Glue the stars to the underside of a plate.

3. Punch holes into the remaining cutouts.

4. Tie string to the cutouts and tape to the inside of the plate (a).

5. Make a hole in the middle of the plate with the sharpened pencil point.

6. Tie a paper clip to a piece of cord.

7. To hang the mobile, push the cord through the hole on the inside in the plate up to the paper clip (b).

BALLOON

SUPPLIES: Heavy cardboard, scissors, glue, pencil, large round balloon, cord, construction paper, ribbon.

1. Glue two long cardboard rectangles together to form a cross.

2. Make a hole in the middle of the cross with a sharpened pencil.

3. Blow up a balloon. Knot the neck.

4. Push the neck through the hole.

5. To make zigzag ropes, cut slits into long narrow paper strips, first on one side, then on the other (study the diagram). Open.

6. Tape ropes and ribbon to the underside of the cardboard.

7. To hang the mobile, tie cord to the neck of the balloon.

POLE

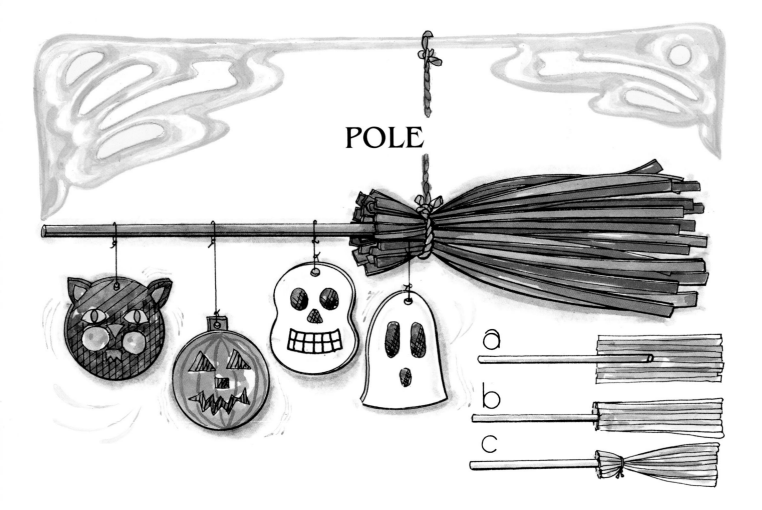

SUPPLIES: Broom handle or dowel, construction paper, scissors, cord, crayons or markers, paper punch, string.

1. Cut many long, narrow paper strips.

2. Lay an end of a broom handle on the strips (a). Bring some strips over the end (b).

3. Tie the strips tightly to the handle with cord to make a broom (c).

4. Draw Halloween characters on paper. Cut out.

5. Punch holes into the cutouts for hanging.

6. With string, tie the characters to the handle.

7. To hang the mobile, tie cord to the broom at the point where it hangs straight.

ANIMATION

LIMBS

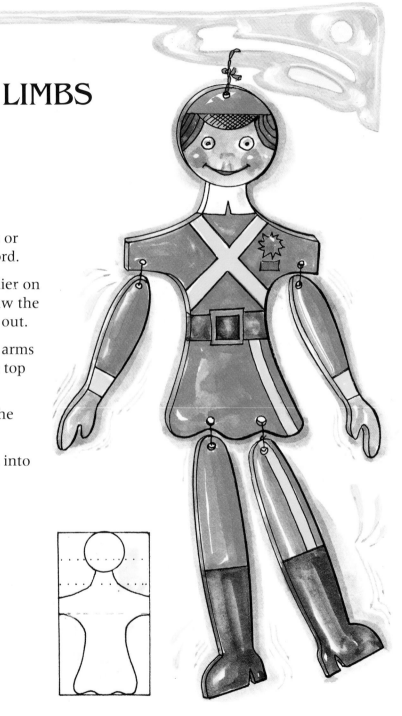

SUPPLIES: Construction paper, crayons or markers, scissors, paper punch, string, cord.

1. Draw the body and head of a toy soldier on paper. The diagram shows how to draw the basic shape. Draw arms and legs. Cut out.

2. Punch holes into the body where the arms and legs will be. Punch holes into the top of the arms and legs.

3. With string, tie the arms and legs to the body.

4. To hang, tie cord into a hole punched into the hat.

JOINTS

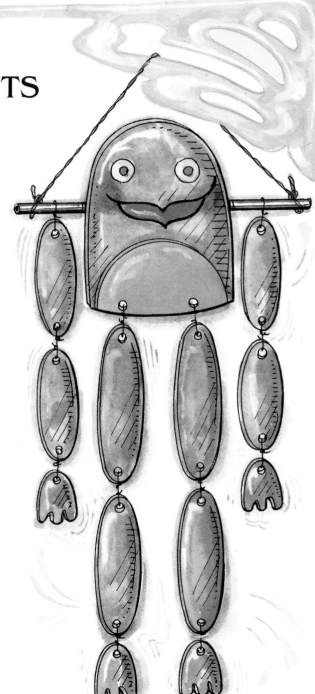

SUPPLIES: Construction paper, pencil, crayons or markers, scissors, paper punch, plastic straw, tape, string, cord.

1. Draw a frog's body on paper to fit on a straw (study the drawing). Cut out.

2. Draw each arm and leg in two sections as shown in the drawing. Draw two hands and two feet. Cut out.

3. Tape a straw to the back of the body.

4. Tie arms and legs together with string.

5. Punch two holes into the bottom of the frog's body.

6. Tie the legs to the body.

7. Tie the arms to the straw.

8. To hang, tie cord to the ends of the straw.

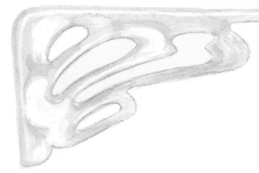

TAILS

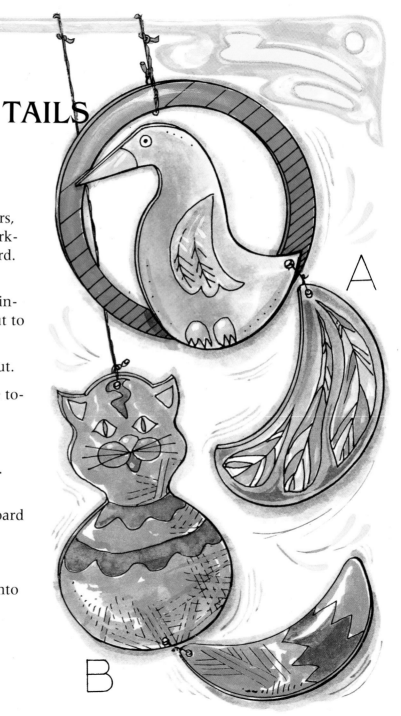

SUPPLIES: Poster board, compass, scissors, construction paper, pencil, crayons or markers, paper punch, string, glue or paste, cord.

BIRD (A)

1. With a compass draw two circles, one inside the other, on poster board. Cut out to form a ring.

2. Draw a bird and a tail on paper. Cut out.

3. Punch a hole into the bird and tail. Tie together with string.

4. Glue the bird on the ring.

5. To hang, tie cord to the top of the ring.

CAT (B)

1. Draw a cat's body and tail on poster board or paper.

2. Attach the tail to the cat (see Bird).

3. To hang, tie string to a hole punched into the top of the head.

A

B

FACES

SUPPLIES: Poster board, ruler, pencil, crayons or markers, compass, scissors, paper punch, tape, string.

1. With a ruler and pencil, draw a large, long rectangle on poster board. Cut out.

2. Draw characters on the rectangle, leaving space at both ends for tabs. The heads are large circles without faces. Draw hats.

3. Carefully cut out the circles (a).

4. For each character, cut out a paper head to fit inside the cutout circle. Draw a different face on each side.

5. Punch a hole into the top of each head. Tie string to each.

6. Tape the string for each head to its matching cutout at the backside of the drawing (b).

7. To stand, fold back the end tabs.

PORTHOLES

SUPPLIES: Green poster board, compass, scissors, construction paper, pencil, tape, string, glue or paste, paper punch, and cord.

1. For leaves, draw a large circle on poster board with a compass. Cut out with a wavy line. Also cut out a wedge (triangle).

2. Draw a circle in the middle of the leaves. Draw smaller circles around it. Cut out.

3. Punch a hole above the wedge and circles.

4. Cut out a paper tree trunk to fit in the wedge. Punch a hole into the point.

5. Tie the trunk to the leaves with string.

6. Draw two matching shapes for the pears and the partridge. They should fit inside the cutout circles.

7. Tape string to one of each two matching shapes (a). Glue the shapes together (b).

8. Tie the pears and the partridge to the cutout circles.

9. To hang, tie cord to the top of the tree.

46

BLOCKS

SUPPLIES: Poster board or construction paper, pencil, ruler, scissors, crayons or markers, glue or paste, paper punch, string, buttons, plastic straws, cord.

1. Cut three long rectangles from poster board. They should all be the same size.

2. Mark off a small section on each rectangle for a tab (arrow in a). Divide the rest of the rectangle into four equal parts.

3. Draw scenery across each rectangle, moving from one to the other (a).

4. To form boxes, fold along the lines with the tabs on the inside. Glue in place (b).

5. Cut paper strips for handles. Punch a hole in the middle of each.

6. Glue the handles to the inside of the boxes (arrow in c).

7. Tie a button to each of the three strings. Feed each string through the hole on the handle (d).

8. Pinch the end of a straw and push it into the end of another straw.

9. Tie the boxes to the double straws (e).

10. To hang, tie cord to the ends of the straw.

SHADOW BOX

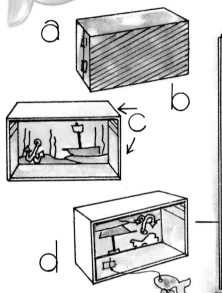

SUPPLIES: Cereal box, tape, scissors, pencil, construction paper, glue or paste, crayons or markers, paper punch, string, sand, small seashells.

1. Tape the open end of a cereal box closed (a).

2. Cut away the front (shaded area in b).

3. Trace the box's sides and top on paper. Cut out.

4. Glue the cutouts on the box (arrows in c).

5. Cut paper to fit inside the box. Draw an ocean scene.

6. Glue the scene to the inside of the box (c).

7. Draw sea creatures on paper. Cut out.

8. Punch holes into each creature. Tie string into the holes.

9. Tape the strings to the top inside the box (d). Add sand and seashells.

FRAME

SUPPLIES: Cereal box, tape, construction paper, pencil, scissors, ruler, glue or paste, paper punch, string.

1. Tape the open end of a cereal box closed (a).

2. Trace all sides of the box on paper. Cut out.

3. Glue the cutouts on the box.

4. Draw a window on both papers with a ruler and pencil (shaded area in a).

5. Cut out the windows (b).

6. Glue the remaining sides on the box (c).

7. Draw wavy water on paper to fit across the bottom of the box. Cut out.

8. Glue the water inside the box.

9. Draw a sailboat, clouds, birds, and sun on paper. Cut out.

10. Punch holes into each cutout. Tie string into each hole.

11. Tape strings to the top inside the box.

DIORAMA

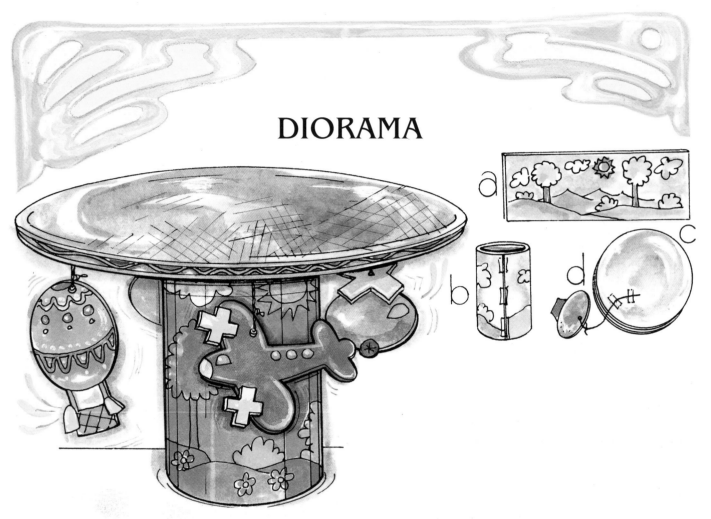

SUPPLIES: Poster board or construction paper, scissors, crayons or markers, tape, heavy cardboard, compass, paper punch, string, tape.

1. Draw a country scene on a long paper rectangle (a).

2. Roll the paper. Tape in place (b).

3. Draw a large circle on cardboard with a compass (c). Cut out.

4. Draw an airplane, helicopter, hot air balloon, and a zeppelin on paper. Cut out.

5. Punch a hole in each aircraft. Tie string into each hole.

6. Tape the strings on one side of the circle toward the edge (d). The aircraft should be equally spaced.

7. Rest the circle on the rolled paper, with the aircraft circulating the landscape.

SUSPENSION ARM

SUPPLIES: Construction paper, scissors, crayons or markers, tape, glue or paste, small can, salt, wire, paper punch, string.

1. Cut a long paper rectangle.

2. Draw grass along the bottom of the paper. Draw flower stems with leaves up to the top of the paper (a).

3. Roll the paper. Tape in place (b).

4. Draw flowers on paper. Cut out.

5. Glue a flower to the top of each stem (c).

6. Cut a piece of wire that will stand higher than the rolled paper.

7. Bend one end of the wire into a curve. Make a loop at the end of the curve.

8. Stand a can filled with salt inside the rolled paper.

9. Push the wires straight end into the can (d).

10. Draw a butterfly on paper. Cut out.

11. Punch holes in the butterfly, tie string into the holes, and hang on the wire.

STORY

SUPPLIES: Colored poster board, pencil, scissors, construction paper, crayons or markers, glue or paste, plastic straw, paper punch, string, cord.

1. Draw an ark's roof, cabin, hull (bottom of boat), and windows on poster board as shown.

2. Glue the cutouts together to form the ark.

3. Draw animals on paper to fit on the ark. Draw fish and a bird. Cut out.

4. Glue the animals to the ark.

5. Punch holes into the fish and bird. Punch holes into the bottom of the ark.

6. Tie the fish to the ark with string.

7. Tape a straw to the back of the ark at one side.

8. Tie the bird to the straw with string.

9. To hang, punch two holes into the roof. Tie cord into the holes.

STREAMERS

SCARECROW

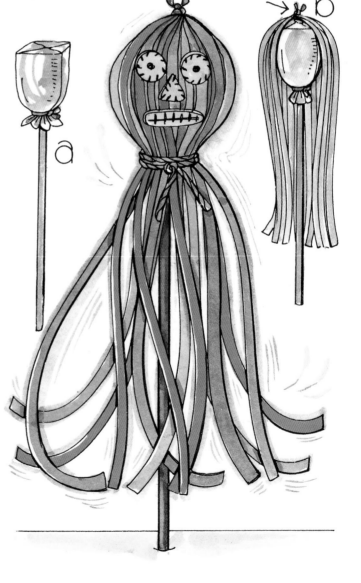

SUPPLIES: Broom handle or straight tree branch, sandwich-size paper bag, newspaper, cord, rolls of crepe-paper streamers, scissors, construction paper, crayon, glue or paste.

1. Place an end of a broom handle inside a bag. Firmly stuff the bag with crumpled newspaper around the handle.

2. Tie the bag to the handle with a cord (a).

3. Cut streamers twice as long as the pole.

4. Gather the streamers. Tie them together in the middle (arrow in b).

5. Place the tied streamers on the bag (b).

6. Arrange the streamers around the bag. Tie them to the handle with cord.

7. Glue on paper eyes, nose, and mouth.

8. To stand, push the pole into the ground.

GHOST

SUPPLIES: White poster board, scissors, package of white crepe paper or tissue paper, stuffing like newspaper or tissue paper, crayon or marker, stapler, paper punch, cord.

1. Cut a sheet of poster board in half, making two rectangles of the same size.

2. Make a ghost by cutting one end of a rectangle into a curve (a). Trace around the curve on the other rectangle. Cut out.

3. Draw a face on each ghost.

4. Cut a piece of crepe paper as wide as the ghost. Cut slits to form a fringe (b).

5. Glue the fringe to the bottom of a ghost (c). Place a little stuffing in the middle (d).

6. Staple the ghosts together with the fringe between them.

7. To hang, punch a hole into the top of the ghost. Tie cord into the hole.

PIÑATA

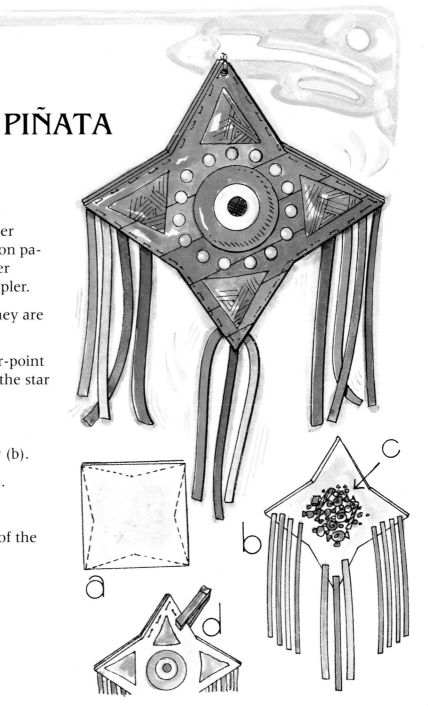

SUPPLIES: Two sheets of colored poster board, ruler, pencil, scissors, construction paper, glue or paste, ribbon or crepe-paper streamer, wrapped candy, tiny toys, stapler.

1. Cut two sheets of poster board so they are square.

2. With a ruler and pencil, draw a four-point star on a square (a). Cut out. Trace the star on the other square. Cut out.

3. Glue paper designs on the stars.

4. Glue ribbons to the back of one star (b).

5. Place wrapped candy on the star (c).

6. Staple the stars together (d).

7. To hang, punch a pole into the top of the piñata. Tie cord into the hole.

RIBBON BANNERS

SUPPLIES: Crepe-paper streamers, scissors, broom handle or dowel for pole, glue or paste, wire coat hanger.

BANNER FLAG (A)

1. Cut streamers the same size.

2. Wrap and glue one end of the streamers around a pole, near one end.

3. To stand, push the pole into the ground.

GARDEN PARTY FLAG (B)

1. Open and bend a wire coat hanger into the shape shown.

2. Glue short streamers or ribbons of the same size to the wire as shown.

3. To stand, push the wire into the ground.

Fabric ribbons make more durable displays. For inclement weather, bring flags inside, or simply use them on special occasions.

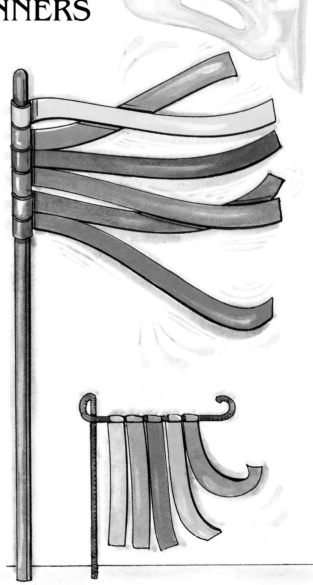

LANTERN

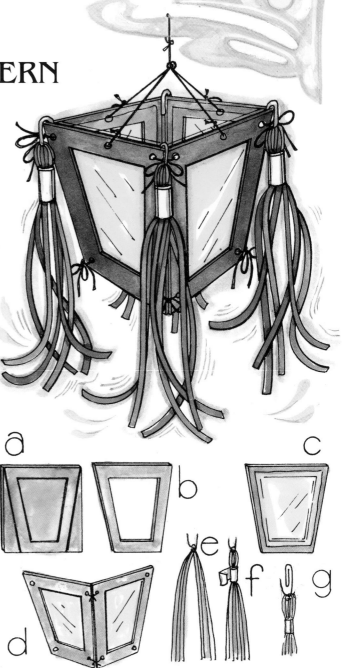

SUPPLIES: Poster board, ruler, pencil, scissors, tissue paper, glue or paste, paper punch, cord, paper ribbon, paper clips.

1. Cut a sheet of poster board into four rectangles the same size.

2. With a ruler and pencil, draw a slanted frame on a rectangle (study a). Cut out (b). Trace the frame on the other rectangles. Cut out.

3. Glue tissue paper on the frames over the openings (c).

4. Punch a hole into all the corners (d).

5. Tie the frames together with string through the holes (d).

6. For tassels, gather ribbons and tie them together at the middle (e). Wrap a small paper strip around the ribbons as shown (f). Glue.

7. Hook a slightly opened paper clip into the top of each tassel (g).

8. Hook the tassels on the lantern's corners.

9. To hang, punch a hole into the top of each frame. Tie cord into the top holes.

MEDALLION

SUPPLIES: Poster board, compass or large dish, construction paper, scissors, glue or paste, crayons or markers, paper punch, string, ribbon.

1. Draw a large circle on poster board with a compass. Cut out.

2. Draw a smaller circle on paper. Cut out. Draw a half-moon face on the small circle (a).

3. Glue the moon centered on the circle to form a medallion (b).

4. Cut away the area around the face (c).

5. Punch holes for the tassel and the star (d).

6. Draw a small star inside a star. Cut out.

7. Tie the star to the medallion.

8. Make a large ribbon tassel as described in Lantern. Tie it to the medallion.

9. To hang, punch a hole into the top of the medallion. Thread cord through the hole and tie.

MAYPOLE

SUPPLIES: Corrugated cardboard, bathroom tissue tube, strong tape, construction paper, glue or paste, pencil, crepe-paper streamers, broom handle or curtain rod for pole.

1. Draw a large circle on cardboard. Cut out.

2. Tape a tube to the middle of the circle (a).

3. Draw leaves and a flower on paper. Cut out.

4. Glue the flower and leaves on the side of the circle without the tube (b).

5. Make holes into the circle between the leaves (b). Use a sharpened pencil with a twisting motion.

6. Tie string to the ends of long streamers (c). Tie the streamers to the circle.

7. To stand, push a pole into the ground. Place the tube on the top of the pole.

A short maypole is decorative. A real maypole requires a tall pole.

SUN CATCHERS

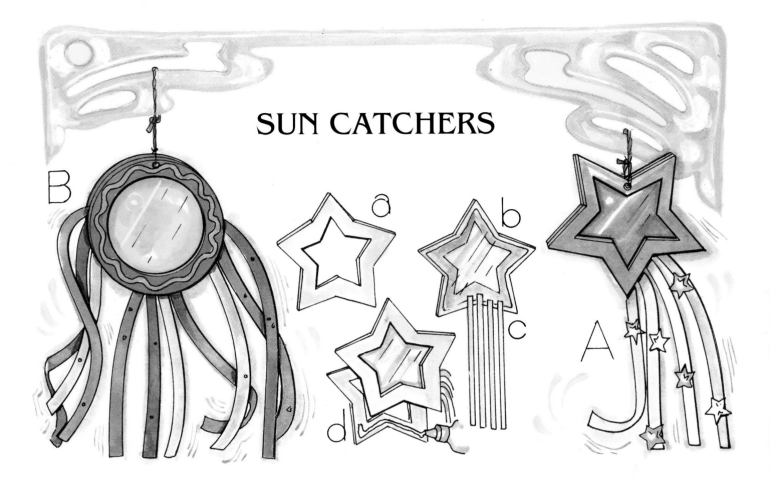

SUPPLIES: Construction paper, pencil, compass, scissors, tissue paper, ribbon, paper punch, string, lick-on stars.

SHOOTING STAR (A)

1. Draw a star inside a star on paper. Cut out (a). Trace the star on paper. Cut out.

2. Glue colored tissue on one star over the opening (b). You can also color white tissue with a marker (b).

3. Glue ribbons to the star (c).

4. Glue the two stars together (d).

5. Add lick-on stars to the ribbons.

6. To hang, punch a hole into the star. Tie cord into the hole.

SUN RAYS (B)

Construct the sun as you did the Shooting Star.

WIND SOCKS

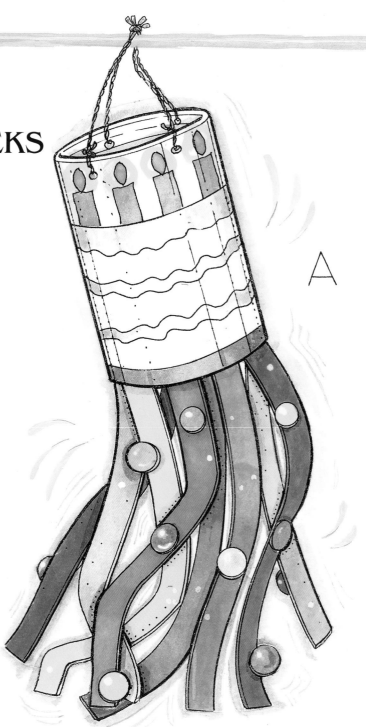

A

SUPPLIES: Poster board, crayons or markers, construction paper, crepe-paper streamers, glue, paper punch, cord.

BIRTHDAY CAKE (A)

1. Cut a long rectangle of poster board.

2. Draw frosting, candles, and a dish on the rectangle (a).

3. Glue streamers to the back, along the bottom (b).

4. Roll into a cylinder (c). Glue in place.

5. Glue paper circles on the streamers.

6. To hang, punch three or four holes equally spaced along the top (d). Reinforce the holes. Tie cord into the holes.

Wind socks can hang from a tree, pole, or line. Fabric ribbon can replace crepe-paper streamers. For inclement weather, bring the wind sock inside.

HALLOWEEN PUMPKIN (B)

Orange sock with orange and black streamers.

62

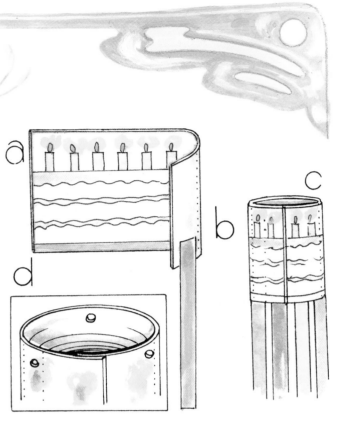

WATER WORLD (C)
Light blue, light green, or white sock with green streamers. Add glitter.

FLOWER GARDEN (D)
Light blue or white sock with streamers in sunshine colors.

CAN OF PEAS (E)
Any color of sock with light green streamers. Draw peas.

MOUSE (F)
White or grey sock with streamers in bright colors.

GARLAND

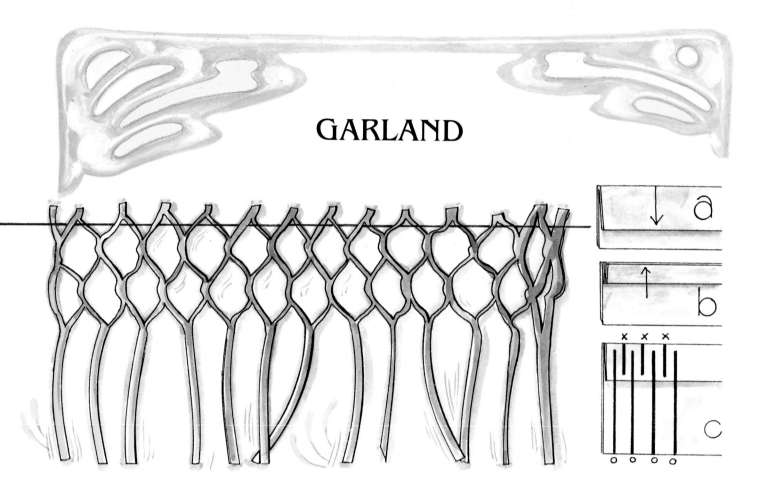

SUPPLIES: Construction paper, scissors, string.

1. Fold over the top of a sheet of paper, ending a little up from the bottom (a).

2. Fold the folded paper back up (b). The edges should line up.

3. The first cut (marked o in c) starts at the bottom. It goes through the entire paper, ending a little away from the top edge.

4. The second cut (marked x in c) starts at the top. It goes through only the folded paper, ending a little away from the bottom edge.

5. Repeat the cuts across the entire paper (c).

6. Unfold the paper. Pull out to expand the garland.

7. To hang, feed cord in and out of the top of the garland.

The closer the cuts, the more tails the garland has and the longer it will be.

SPRAYS

SUPPLIES: Construction paper, crepe-paper streamers, yarn, scissors, paper punch, glitter, glue.

CHAINS (A)
Add ribbon to a chain of glued paper rings. Hang with string.

RIBBONS (B)
Glue glitter designs on streamers. Punch holes with a paper punch.

STREAMERS (C)
Scallop streamers, see Vines on page 66.

PENDANTS (D)
Glue two matching paper shapes together with the end of a piece of yarn between them. Tie several together.

Hang sprays as decorations from everything including an overhead light to a patio umbrella.

VINES

SUPPLIES: Rolls of green crepe-paper streamers, construction paper, crayons or markers, scissors, glue or paste, cord, heavy tape.

1. Cut streamers into lengths that will stretch from the ceiling to the floor or the top of a door to the floor.

2. Place the middle and forefinger of one hand on the edge of a streamer. Force the paper down with your finger, creating a scallop (arrow in the diagram).

3. Make scallops along the edges of all the streamers to create vines.

4. Glue paper leaves, flowers, and insects on the vines.

5. To hang, glue the ends of the vines to cord. Stretch the cord across a room, a corner, or a door. Tape or tie in place.

TURN & SPIN

STRIP WHEELS

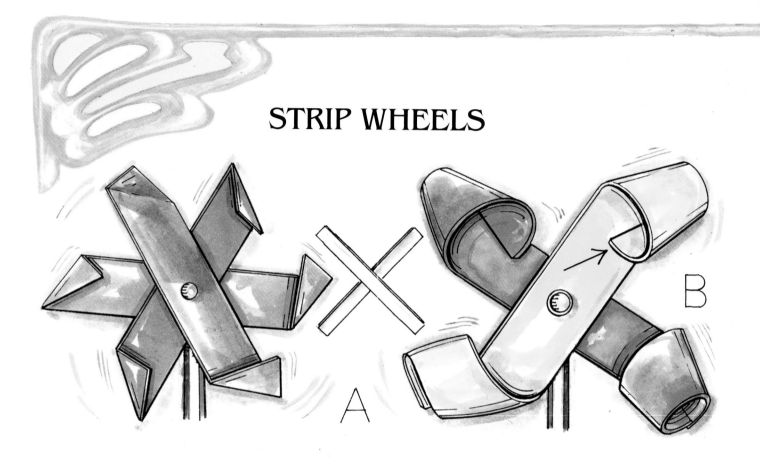

SUPPLIES: Construction paper, scissors, glue or paste, long thin nail, plastic straws or wooden dowel.

STAR (A)

1. Cut three paper strips the same size.

2. Glue the strips together to form a star.

3. Fold over the ends of the strips into triangles, all facing in the same direction.

4. Pinch an end of a straw and push it into the end of another straw.

5. Push a nail into the middle of the star.

6. Push the nail through the straws at one end. Just a little of the point should extend out.

7. To spin, blow at the strip wheel or hold it in the wind.

CRISSCROSS (B)

1. Glue two very long paper strips together to form a cross (see diagram).

2. Curl the ends, facing the same direction.

3. Glue a corner of each curl to the cross (see arrow in the drawing).

4. Attach to a double straw and spin, as described in the Star.

PROPELLER (C)

1. Cut two long paper strips.

2. Punch a hole into the middle of a strip, near the top edge (a).

3. Cut a slit into the middle of each strip, a little more than halfway up (b).

4. Draw designs on the strips.

5. Tie string into the hole (c).

6. Fit the slits into each other (d). To secure, add glue where the strips interlock.

7. When dry, curl the ends of each strip (study e). The curls face the same direction.

8. Hang by the string.

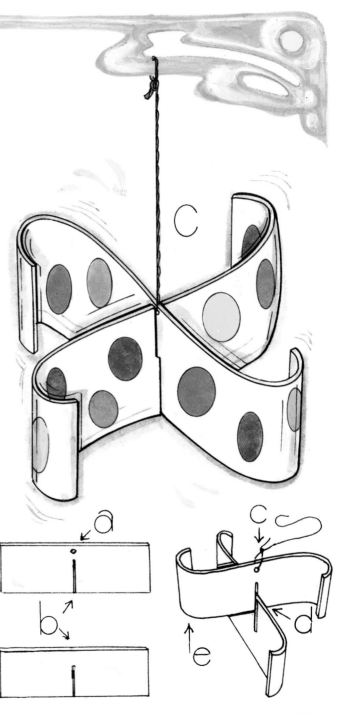

PINWHEELS

SUPPLIES: Construction paper, compass, ruler, pencil, scissors, long thin nail, plastic straws or wooden dowel.

ROUND WHEEL (A)

1. Draw a circle on paper with a compass. Draw a small circle in the middle (study a). Cut out the larger circle.

2. With a ruler and pencil, divide the circle into eight equal sections (a).

3. Cut along the lines up to the circle (b).

4. Cut tiny sideways slits going in the same direction (study the blowup, arrow in b).

5. Fold over the paper along the cut lines to form a wheel.

6. Pinch the end of one straw and push it into the end of another straw.

70

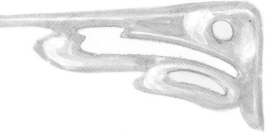

7. Push a nail through the middle of the wheel.

8. Push the nail through the straws at one end. Just a little of the point extends out.

9. To spin, blow at the pinwheel or hold it in the wind.

SQUARE WHEEL (B)

1. Draw a large square on paper with a ruler and pencil. Cut out.

2. Draw lines from corner to corner (c).

3. Cut along the lines more than halfway to the middle (d).

4. Curl over and glue every other corner (marked x in e) to each other.

5. Attach the wheel to a double straw (f) and spin, described in Round Wheel.

TABLE WHEEL (C)

1. Use a compass to draw a circle inside a circle on paper. Cut out the larger circle.

2. Make slanted cuts up to the circle (g).

3. Curl a side of each section, to form a wheel (h). The curls face the same direction.

4. Twist a sharpened pencil through the center of the wheel, on the side with the curls (i). Remove the pencil.

5. To spin, place the wheel on a flat surface, curls facing up. Blow on the wheel.

The wheel spins on the paper pushed through the hole.

g   h   i

C

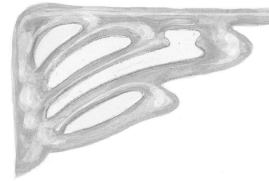

BLADES

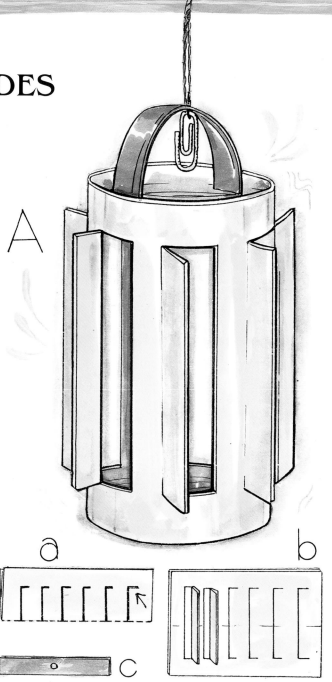

SUPPLIES: Paper, scissors, glue or paste, paper punch, button or paper clip, string or cord.

CYLINDER (A)

1. Fold a sheet of paper in half along the length.

2. Make cuts into the folded edge, ending a little away from the opposite edge (a).

3. Cut short sideways slits in the same direction (study arrow in a).

4. Open the paper. Fold along the cuts to form blades (b).

5. Roll the paper into a cylinder. Glue.

6. Cut a narrow paper strip. Punch a hole into the middle (c).

7. Glue the ends of the strip to the inside of the cylinder, forming a loop.

8. To hang, tie a paper clip to string. Feed the string through the hole in the loop.

CONE (B)

1. Roll a very long strip of paper into a ring. Glue.

2. Draw a long, narrow triangle on paper. Cut out. Trace the triangle many times on paper. Cut out.

3. Fold over a corner of each triangle (study a and b). The folds are on the same side.

4. With the folds facing out, glue the tops of the triangles around the ring (c). Dry.

5. Glue the bottom points (arrow in c) together to form a cone.

6. Hang like the Cylinder.

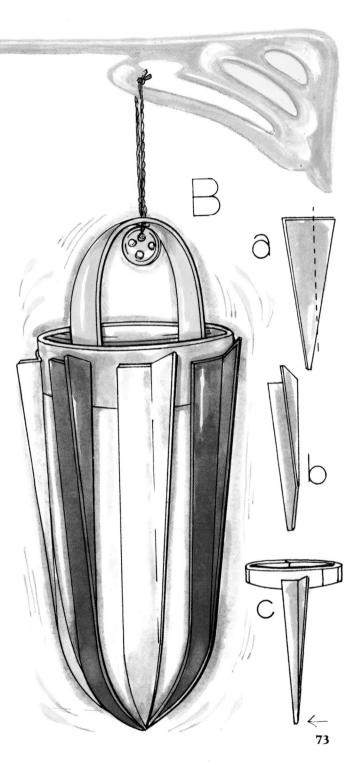

73

PADDLES

SUPPLIES: Two paper plates, glue, bead or paper clip, construction paper, scissors, large nail, cord.

1. Glue the underside of two plates together (a). Dry.

2. Make a hole in the center of the glued plates. Use a nail with a twisting motion (b).

3. Cut six slits through the rims of both plates (c). They should be equally spaced.

4. Cut six paper rectangles the same size. They should be longer than the slits.

5. Curl an end of each rectangle (d).

6. Fit the rectangles into the slits. The curled ends face the same direction (e).

7. To hang, tie a button to a piece of string. Feed the string through the hole.

RIBS

SUPPLIES: Paper, scissors, glue or paste, paper punch, button or paper clip, string or cord.

1. Fold a sheet of paper in half along the length.

2. Cut the short sides at a slant (study the shaded areas in a).

3. Make cuts into the folded edge following the slant of the sides (study b).

4. Unfold and roll the paper into a cylinder (c). Glue in place at the top and bottom.

5. Cut a narrow strip of paper. Punch a hole in the middle.

6. Glue the ends of the strip inside the top opening of the cylinder, forming a loop.

7. To hang, tie string to a button. Feed the string through the hole in the loop.

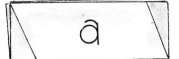

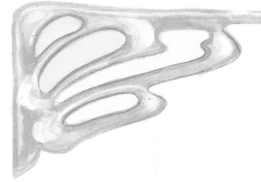

CUPS

SUPPLIES: Construction paper, ruler, pencil, scissors, glue or paste, paper punch, button or paper clip, string.

OPEN CUPS (A)

1. With a ruler and pencil, draw a square on paper. Cut out. Trace the square several times on paper. Cut out.

2. Glue opposite corners of the squares together to form open cups (a and b).

3. Roll two long paper strips of the same size into rings (c). Glue each closed.

4. Glue the top points of the cups around one ring (d). Dry.

5. Glue the bottom points around the other ring (arrows in e). Dry.

6. Cut a narrow paper strip. Punch a hole in the middle.

7. Glue the ends of the strip to the inside of the ring to form a loop.

8. To hang, tie a button to string. Feed the string through the hole in the loop.

POINTED CUPS (B)

1. Cut long paper rectangles.

2. Bring the top corners toward the middle of each rectangle (a). Crisscross the corners of each to form pointed cups (b). Glue in place.

3. Roll a strip of paper into a ring. Glue closed.

4. Glue the cups around the ring, facing in the same direction. Glue on the cups' criss-crossed sides.

5. Add a loop to the ring and hang as described in Open Cups.

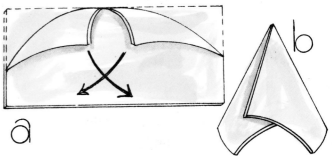

SCOOP

SUPPLIES: Cardboard, scissors, compass, construction paper, glue or paste, plastic straws, tape, string.

1. Draw large circles of the same size on different colored papers. The circles should be as wide as a straw is long. Draw two smaller circles. Cut out.

2. Glue the smaller circles on the larger circles (a). Mix the colors.

3. Tape a straw on the back of a circle, across the middle (b).

4. Glue the circles together (c). Press flat.

5. Feed string through the straw (d).

6. Curl the top and bottom of the circle, each in a different direction.

7. To make a frame, draw a circle in the middle of a cardboard square. It should be larger than the paper circle. Cut out.

8. Place the paper circle inside the cutout circle. Tape the string in place (f).

9. To hang, tie string into holes punched into the top of the frame.

When the scoop spins fast, the colors on both sides blend into a single color.

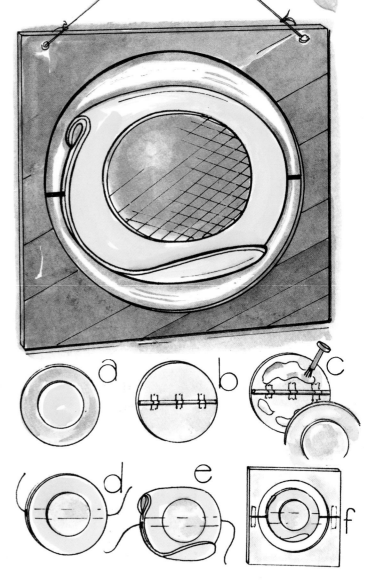

78

VANE

SUPPLIES: Paper cups, scissors, pencil, compass, cardboard, tape, plastic straws, poster board, construction paper, glue or paste.

1. Draw a large circle on cardboard with a compass. Cut out.

2. Make a hole in the bottom of two cups in the center (a). Use a sharpened pencil.

3. Cut one cup in half (b).

4. Tape the bottom half to the middle of the circle (c). The hole faces up.

5. Place the other cup over the cup on the circle (d).

6. Pinch an end of a straw and push it into an end of another straw.

7. Fit the double straw into the holes of both cups (see dotted lines in e).

8. Draw an arrow on poster board. Cut out.

9. Tape the arrow near its point to the straw.

10. Glue a paper "N" (north), "S" (south), "E" (east) and "W" (west), on the circle. Follow the order shown in the drawing.

11. To turn, set the vane in the wind. Line up "N" with north.